OPPOSITES OF EACH OTHER

OPPOSITES of EACH OTHER

Langston Brown-McFadden

Opposites of Each Other
© 2024 Langston Brown-McFadden
ISBN: 979-8-9893829-3-4

Published by Mama's Kitchen Press
Austin, TX / Los Angeles, CA
mamaskitchenpress.com

First Trade Paperback Original Edition, 2024

Manufactured in the United States of America

Cover painting by Langston Brown-McFadden
Cover design & layout design by Emily Anne Evans

CONTENTS

FOREWORD

Langston,
What a powerful name
Your light has always proven to never dim
You are me and I am you
You made me a Boy mom
You taught me patience and resilience
You loved me when I was broken
Took all my pieces and made me whole again
I love you until infinity
When you are lost
Like a lighthouse
Remember I will always be home
Like the North Star
Follow me
When you feel fatigued
Lost
Remember I will always give you my strength
As you gave me yours without knowing

I love you son and I am so proud of you. You are truly amazing and remind me each day to be grateful even when times are difficult. When you were four years old and could not speak— as everyone else worried I knew that you were waiting on your time. This collection of poems is only a small look into a voice you are still finding on your own time.

Love,
Mom

CHAPTER 1

Separation and Together

As sun shines and brings the day

I, the moon just walk away

As I sleep every night there's one day

when we meet again and make an eclipse

When God made us he wanted two deities

to make people and bring them back

So he made life and death

Even when life brought creatures to earth

it also brought separation

And as death guided the souls of earth

death to God

When we are young

we don't know that our time is limited

But as we age

our time is shortened

Or you're just getting closer to God

When Jesus was put on the cross

He still wanted to show mercy

But when we did nothing to the devil

he decided to attack us

CHAPTER 2

Emotions

As fear controls us when we are afraid

we tend to run

or try to fight our way out

When we think bravery

we usually think boldness

But we forget

that bravery is when we cast away fear

Joy is an emotion we all have in our early emotions

But when we go through stress

we forget about joy

Sadness is an emotion

that helps us communicate with people under stress

But also helps us better understand them

CHAPTER 3

Time and Growth

As we are young

we face a life of fun

But when we lose that sense of fun in our life

we start to lose curiosity

When we lose both of those from our childhood

we start to face loneliness

But if we allow people in our lives

we will be whole again

When we grow

we seem to forget about curiosity

But curiosity is what helps us discover new things

CHAPTER 4

Animals

As birds soar through the sky

As the sun rises

bats come out to play

But I, the owl

look for prey

But it will be soon time for day

and now it is time for me to play

As the night rests

the sun awakens

As the Savannah shows the lions waking roar

the sparrows fly to get food

As the lion hunts his prey with his brother

they ran and became tired

As they start to fall asleep

they had no fear

As we are young tigers

we love to sleep and play

But as we age

we learn dedication

As monkeys swing

the trees rustle

A bird flies through the jungle

As the bird had to meet with his friend

mongol

they met, they had time

Hello

This is Joe

Joe likes to go slow

but Joe can't go fast

because he is a sloth that's always last

So Joe tried and tried to go fast

As he closed his eyes

he opened them and was surprised

he was going fast

he was no longer last

CHAPTER 5

Mental Peace

As we dream

we use imagination to power our dreams

But when we are scared

that is what fuels nightmares

But if we continue to grow our minds

we continue growing our imagination

When the rhythm is in our mind

we feel the sense of relaxation

But when our rhythm is broken

we feel as if our body has been split

into several pieces

As we dream

we feel the stress leave our body

as we drift through dreams we had in the past

But as we start to dive in

we must wake up

As the darkness of terror starts to flow into my mind

it starts to corrupt my dreams

As it starts to chase you and catches up

he catches you

you wake up in fear

I was falling into an ocean

as clear as the sky

When I fell

all fear left my mind

As I reached the surface

I felt renewed

As I came ashore

I felt calm in my mind

When the heat of lava

is near the skin

it burns

As volcanoes start to erupt

chaos boils beneath the earth

which is like our anger

CHAPTER 6

Body Positivity and Negativity

As we admire other people

we put negativity on ourselves

and we try to make ourselves look like who we are not

We should instead

just be ourselves

When we admire ourselves

we feel good about ourselves

and we try to make ourselves look even better

But all we need is someone to comfort us

CHAPTER 7

Mental Positivity and Negativity

As we poison our mind

with false information

It continues to flow through our mind

like water

Seeping into the ground

making us hate past things we like

and making us do what we usually don't do

Which leaves us to hate

When we clear our mind

we feel balance

As we continue to feel balance

but more like water

Until we start to break that balance

CHAPTER 8

Nature

We as people

want to know what it's like

to be a tree

But instead we poison them

We try again to copy that exact tree

but I know none can't be like thee

For I am like a tree

Each tree is different

and unique

For I am like a tree

cannot copy thee

When we as people

grow from the seed we were born as

and use our knowledge to grow

Our petals of intelligence and each petal

is different in a unique way

Like each person in the world

CHAPTER 9

Population

Our body is like the ocean

made of 70% water

Like the ocean

we can change the tides of time

As even the fall of a leaf

can change the ripple of time

When we allow poison to enter our body

it damages it

mentally and physically

When we pollute

we pollute our air

There would be nothing to spare

You'll start to lose air

which is something as people

we cannot bare

We love our gorgeous hair

CHAPTER 10

Betrayal and Friends

Betrayal is the key to heartbreak

which makes our fate fatal

for our mental and physical health

Friendship is like a fire

It grows bigger the longer you are with it

But when you put that light out

you have nothing to guide you in the darkness

For life can give you friends

life can also give you enemies

If you choose to make your enemies into friends

You shall get the good of life

CHAPTER 11

There Are No Differences

As long as people have existed

there have always been alliances

Some use alliances

even if they're at disagreement

They continue to work together

forever

Soaring through the skies

Scales as thick as armor

As hot as anger

for it has had its hardships as well

If we treat beasts not like people

As people hunt beasts, we think they're not like people

but we forget that we are also like animals

The pets we have in our home are like people

they think like people

some act like people

They have their own minds as well

So we must trust in our little buddies

with our lives

and theirs

In the whispering woods where shadows play

animals roam in their graceful ballet

A deer with eyes filled with pools of amber

that tell the story of night

Against the backdrop of a sun-drenched field

a shepard stands with heart unsealed

His dog

a companion for life

with the eyes of a rising sun

On my 9th year of surviving

I met an animal

Her hair as dark as night

but beautiful as a sunrise at its peak

It guided me to the light

I seeked, but when I found that light turns out

she was the guardian angel of my life

But when my guardian angel was taken

it felt like my light will never waken

But then I remembered the good times we had

I know you wouldn't want me to be sad

So I choose to keep you by my side

So now I will never hide

ABOUT THE AUTHOR

Langston is a 12-year-old writer and art enthusiast. He enjoys art in all of its forms and uses every day as a place to play and imagine. This collection of poems is his first published work and a place where he has rooted his writing capabilities. Follow Langston on Instagram @blackboyspaint.

mamaskitchenpress.com

Mama's Kitchen Press believes that stories affirm our humanity. It is our mission to publish stories that are personal, heartfelt, and intimate.

youthwriterscamp.com

This book was created as part of Youth Writer's Camp, a program that follows a 10-Week Social-Emotional Curriculum promoting positive mental health, educational, and economic outcomes among youth.

The aim of Youth Writer's Camp is to:
• Teach adaptive social and emotion regulation skills
• Improve effective communication skills
• Increase literacy skills through creative written expression
• Empower youth by amplifying their voices to tell their stories
• Support each youth in becoming a published writer

www.ingramcontent.com/pod-product-compliance
Lightning Source LLC
Chambersburg PA
CBHW060509300726
48975CB00008B/2705